LIVING WELL

LIVING WITH CEREBRAL PALSY

by Susan H. Gray

THE CHILD'S WORLD®
CHANHASSEN, MINNESOTA

The publisher wishes to sincerely thank George Pugh, M.D., and Collin Pugh, who himself is Living Well with cerebral palsy, for their help in preparing this book for publication.

Published in the United States of America by The Child's World®
P.O. Box 326
Chanhassen, MN 55317-0326
800-599-READ
www.childsworld.com

Photo Credits: Cover: Picturequest/Corbis, Custom Medical Stock Photo, Inc. (inset); Lowell Georgia/Corbis: 24 (top); Picturequest/Corbis: 1; Custom Medical Stock Photo, Inc.: 20, 25; Dan Dempster/Dembinsky Photo Associates: 11; Richard Hamilton Smith/Dembinsky Photo Associates: 16; GettyImages: 29; The Image Bank/GettyImages: 17; Miramax Films, Courtesy of GettyImages: 19; Stone/Getty Images: 10, 18; Susan Gray: 14, 27; Kennedy Krieger Institute: 21; Tami Payton: 5; Myrleen Cates/PhotoEdit: 12, 13; Myrleen Ferguson: 26; Tony Freeman/PhotoEdit: 7; Robert Ginn/PhotoEdit: 9; Richard Hutchings: 15; Robin L. Sachs: 24 (bottom); Jeff Green/Unicorn: 9, 23

The Child's World®: Mary Berendes, Publishing Director

Editorial Directions, Inc.: E. Russell Primm, Editor; Alice Flanagan, Photo Researcher; Linda S. Koutris, Photo Selector; The Design Lab, Designer and Page Production; Red Line Editorial, Fact Researcher; Irene Keller, Copy Editor; Tim Griffin/IndexServ, Indexer; Donna Frassetto, Proofreader

Library of Congress Cataloging-in-Publication Data
Gray, Susan H.
 Living with cerebral palsy / by Susan H. Gray.
    p. cm. — (Living Well series)
Includes index.
 ISBN 1-56766-101-7
 1. Cerebral palsy—Juvenile literature. [1. Cerebral palsy.] I. Title. II. Series.
RC388 .G74 2002
 362.1'96836—dc21   2002002865

TABLE OF CONTENTS

CHAPTER ONE

Do You Know Someone Who Has Cerebral Palsy?

Tanner and Taylor love to play soccer. As twin brother and sister, they do a lot of things together. They ride horseback at a nearby farm. In the summer, they spend long, hot days in their grandmother's swimming pool. Tanner loves to go fishing with his dad. Taylor likes to make bracelets and necklaces with her little sister. They both have some problems walking. They have to wear braces on their legs. But the braces don't seem to slow them down.

The twins are 2 of about 500,000 people in the United States with cerebral palsy (suh-REE-brul PAWL-zee)—about 1 person out of every 500. Cerebral palsy is often called CP.

Like Tanner and Taylor, these kids love to fish!

CHAPTER TWO

What Is Cerebral Palsy?

Cerebral means having to do with the brain. *Palsy* means weakness or poor control. When the body is working right, the brain and muscles work together. The brain tells the muscles when to tighten up and when to relax. It tells the muscles how to move. But in a person with CP, the brain does not always send the right signals to the muscles. People with CP have a hard time controlling their movements.

There are three main kinds of cerebral palsy—**spastic** (SPASS-tik), athetoid (ATH-uh-toyd), and ataxic (ay-TAX-ik). Spastic CP is the most common. The muscles of people with spastic CP are too tense. Their arms and legs seem stiff. They may have trouble moving their legs to take steps. They might also have a hard time letting go of things. It seems like their muscles just won't relax.

People with spastic CP sometimes need a walker to help them get around.

People with athetoid cerebral palsy have trouble controlling how they move. They might seem to be making faces and looking around a lot. Their arms and legs don't always do what they want them to do. They may have trouble sitting up straight too. Their muscles seem to have a mind of their own.

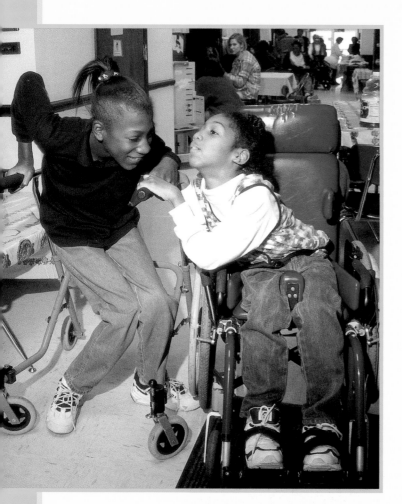

Athetoid CP can cause problems with controlling movement.

People with ataxic cerebral palsy have a hard time with balance. They are not very steady when they walk. Sometimes their hands are shaky. They might have trouble buttoning a shirt or using scissors. Their muscles just aren't very steady.

Some people with cerebral palsy might have trouble with only one arm or one leg. Others might have trouble controlling both arms and both legs or even their whole body. People with CP often have other problems, too. They may not see or hear well. They might have to wear glasses and hearing aids. They may have a hard time learning things in school. Not everyone with CP has these problems though.

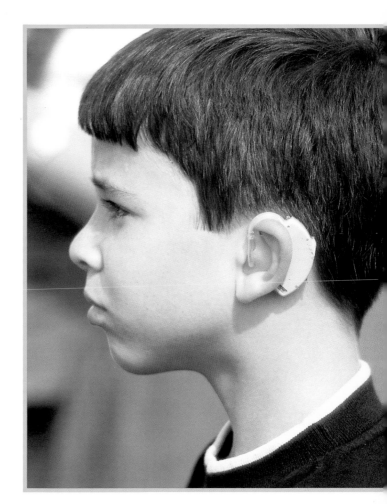

Sometimes CP affects hearing.

Cerebral palsy can be very mild or very severe. People with CP have it all their lives. There is no cure, but people learn how to live with it. Surgery, **therapy,** and medication can sometimes help make life easier for people with CP.

CHAPTER THREE

WHAT CAUSES
CEREBRAL PALSY?

Brain damage in babies causes cerebral palsy. Everyone's brain needs oxygen to work right. Blood has oxygen in it. Blood brings that oxygen to the brain areas that control muscles.

Even before babies are born, their brains need oxygen. If a baby's brain does not get enough oxygen, it will be damaged. That damaged part might never heal. If the damage is in an area that controls muscles, the baby could be born with cerebral palsy.

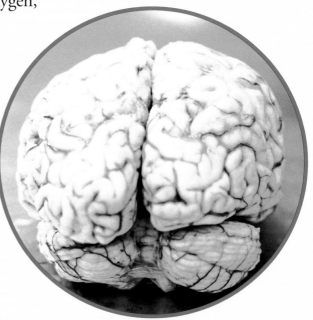

If enough oxygen doesn't get to the brain, it can be damaged. Damage to the area of the brain that controls muscle movement can cause CP.

Sometimes damage to a baby's brain is caused before it is born.

Several other things could cause cerebral palsy. Sometimes a

mother gets a bad illness before her baby is born. Sometimes a baby

does not get enough oxygen at birth. Sometimes a baby is just fine at

Parents keep small objects and toys away from little children so they don't choke. Choking can keep oxygen from the baby's brain and cause CP.

first. Then later the baby may choke on a toy or get hurt in an accident and be unable to breathe for a little while. Any of these things could keep oxygen from getting to the brain. They could be the cause of cerebral palsy.

Doctors cannot be sure that a newborn baby has cerebral palsy. They cannot see it on an X ray. They cannot tell it from a blood test. They have to check on the baby for months. If a baby does not reach, sit up, or walk at a certain age, the baby might have CP.

CHAPTER FOUR

WHAT'S IT LIKE TO HAVE CEREBRAL PALSY?

Everyday tasks can be problems for someone with cerebral palsy. Brushing teeth, eating, dressing, and just getting around can be hard. But people have found all kinds of clever ways to handle these problems.

Toothbrushes, forks, and spoons with big, thick handles are easier for people with CP to hold. Pencils with special rubber grips are easier too. Clothes and shoes with Velcro are also helpful.

The special rubber grip on this girl's pencil helps her write.

Children who have CP might need to wear braces or splints.

These are stiff pieces of plastic that strap on. They go on the ankles,

feet, legs, or even the back. Braces or splints help keep body parts

straight as they grow strong.

A therapist helps this girl with her splint.

Some people use crutches, walkers, or wheelchairs to get around. Walkers are simple metal frames with legs and wheels. A person who uses a walker holds onto it while walking. Many children put a bike basket and a horn on their walkers. At Christmastime,

Crutches help this boy get around the halls of his school.

some kids even decorate their walkers with tinsel and lights!

Wheelchairs let people sit down as they move from place to place. Very often, children with CP have wheelchairs with motors. They control the chair with a joystick, just like a video game. Most

These girls play ball with their friend in a motorized wheelchair.

children get quite good at "driving" their wheelchairs.

Children with cerebral palsy may still have a tough time getting

around, however. They may have trouble walking up stairs and

curbs. They might need ramps instead. Their wheelchairs can get

Ramps help people in wheelchairs get in and out of buildings.

stuck in gravel. And they might have trouble keeping their balance

on ground that is uneven.

On the school playground, swings can be a problem. Children

with cerebral palsy may need swings with backs. The backs help the

Shooting "hoops" with a friend is a great way to get exercise.

children to stay balanced and secure. In a crowded classroom, a student might have trouble getting around with a walker or crutches. And a student in a wheelchair will need a special table or desk.

Kids with cerebral palsy really like to have special friends to help them and play with them. They might work together to decorate the bulletin board.

At lunch, friends may want to carry their cafeteria tray and eat with them. At recess, friends might help them play basketball. Kids in wheelchairs love to "shoot hoops."

A DETERMINED BOY

Before Christy Brown was even one year old, everyone knew something was wrong. He could not control his arms or legs. Only his left foot seemed normal. It was the 1930s. No one knew much about cerebral palsy at that time. The doctor said Christy would never be able to do anything. He said the boy's brain was no good.

Luckily, Christy's mom would not listen to such talk. One day she saw Christy pick up a piece of chalk with his left foot. As he scribbled on the floor, she had an idea. She would teach him to write with his foot! In time, Christy learned to write and also to paint. When he grew up, he wrote the story of his life. He called it *My Left Foot*. Christy Brown kept writing and painting until he died. Today, people still read books written by the boy some people said would never amount to anything.

CHAPTER FIVE

WHAT CAN WE DO ABOUT CEREBRAL PALSY?

Many years ago, no one knew what caused cerebral palsy. No one knew how to help people with CP. Children with cerebral palsy were not allowed to go to school. Some of these children never even got out of the house.

The disease was first studied in the 1800s. A doctor in England began to examine some unusual babies. He noticed they did not develop quite like other babies. For example, they could not pick up their toys. And they did not sit up or walk when other babies did. The doctor thought these babies might not have gotten enough oxygen when they were born. The doctor's name was William J. Little. The illness

Dr. William J. Little

these babies had became

known as Little's disease.

Doctor Little

thought exercises might

help the children. He

was right. When hospital

workers helped the

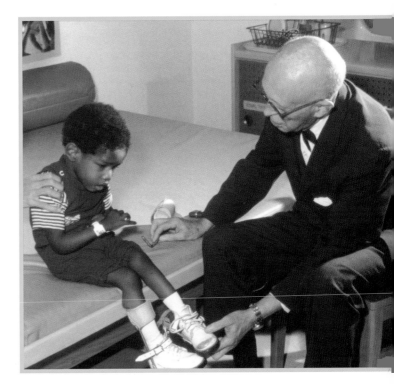

Dr. Winthrop Phelps helps a young child with CP.

children to exercise their arms and legs, the children learned to move

better. They started picking up their toys. With help, some even learned

to walk. This was an exciting new thing. Over the years, hospital

workers thought of more and better exercises. They tried new ways

to help the children move better.

Later, a doctor in the United States became interested. His name

was Winthrop Phelps. When he had patients with Little's disease, he exercised their muscles. He helped them learn to walk and climb stairs. He showed their parents how to help them. In 1937, he started the first **clinic** in the United States just for children with CP. Some of his patients grew up happy and did just fine. Doctor Phelps was the first person to use the term cerebral palsy.

Today, doctors know there are different kinds of CP. And they know all kinds of ways to help these patients. Some medicines and operations are helpful. Doctors give these children medicines that relax spastic muscles. When the drugs wear off, the muscles tighten up again. Doctors can also perform an operation that helps spastic leg muscles relax. But the best thing for most people is therapy.

Most people with cerebral palsy will need a **therapist** (THER-uh-pist) at some time. Therapists are people who teach patients how to do things better. Physical (FIZZ-uh-kuhl) therapists

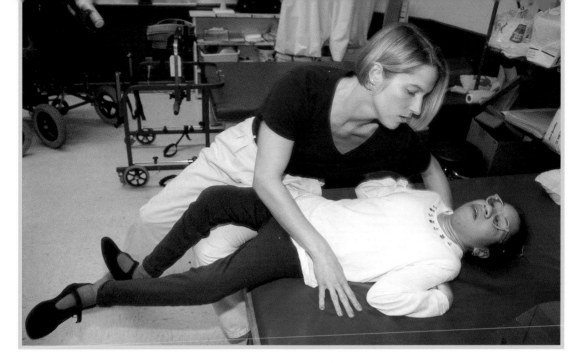

A physical therapist works with her young patient.

show their patients how to do exercises. They help babies to sit up and to crawl. They teach children how to walk and go up stairs. Physical therapists teach people with CP how to use walkers and wheelchairs. They show them how to use playground equipment.

Occupational (ahk-yoo-PAY-shun-uhl) therapists help their patients learn to do everyday tasks. They teach them to brush their hair and dress themselves. They help them use forks, spoons, toothbrushes, and marking pens. They also help them with writing and drawing.

Speech therapists help people to speak better. People with CP

learn to control their lips and tongue and talk more clearly. Some

patients have a very hard time saying their words properly.

They need something to help them. Some

people use little computers with all

kinds of recorded messages. They

just have to push a button and the

A therapist works with a patient who is learning to use a head wand to operate a computer (top left). Another therapist works with young CP patients to control their lips and tongues to speak more clearly (bottom right).

computer does the talking

for them!

Today, many people

with CP enjoy long, happy

lives. Some ride horses for

fun and exercise. Some live

Today, kitchens can be modified to help those in wheelchairs reach things more easily.

in houses that are fixed up just for them. These houses have wide

doorways so that wheelchairs can pass through them. They have

touch-lamps in the rooms. They have big handles on water faucets

and special seats in the showers.

Today, many people with cerebral palsy go to college. A few

even study to be therapists! Things have come a long, long way.

Children with cerebral palsy are no longer stuck in the house for life.

CHAPTER SIX

WILL WE EVER CURE CEREBRAL PALSY?

We are learning more about cerebral palsy all the time. Today, doctors give women special shots before their babies are born.

Pregnant women learn how to eat and exercise properly to help keep their unborn babies healthier.

These shots keep mothers from getting illnesses that might harm the brain of an unborn baby. Also, mothers have learned how to stay healthy and eat right so that their babies are born healthy. Therapists have learned to work with younger and younger children. Inventors are coming up with new and better talking computers.

Scientists

are learning how a baby's brain develops. They are studying the blood and breathing problems that some babies have. They are figuring out how to stop those problems.

Even young children can benefit from working with therapists.

Some doctors are checking to see if medicines help. Other doctors have found that some children with cerebral palsy have differences in their teeth. They are not quite sure what this means. But they are looking into it. Maybe someday we will have all the answers. Maybe someday CP will not be a problem at all.

Glossary

clinic (KLIN-ik) A clinic is a place where people get medical care, but do not stay overnight.

scientist (SYE-uhn-tist) A scientist is someone who studies science and medicine.

spastic (SPAZ-tik) Someone who is spastic is affected with spasms.

therapist (THER-uh-pist) A therapist is someone who treats an illness or injury.

therapy (THER-uh-pee) Therapy is the treatment of an illness or problem.

Questions and Answers about Cerebral Palsy

What is cerebral palsy? Cerebral palsy is a condition of the brain that prevents the muscles and the brain from working together properly.

Can I catch cerebral palsy from somebody? No, that would be impossible. It is okay to hug and play and share your toys with a person who has CP.

My friend at school has cerebral palsy. Will she ever get well? Your friend can get better at doing many things, such as walking, putting on her coat, and coloring. But she will always have CP.

Sometimes I can't understand what she's saying. What should I do? Your friend probably has trouble controlling her lip and tongue muscles. Just be patient and listen very closely to what she says. It's okay to ask her to repeat things. Then give her a little extra time to answer.

What's the hardest part of having CP? Some children say it hurts their feelings when people stare at them or make fun of them. It's also hard when people treat them as if they are not very smart.

Helping a Friend Who Has Cerebral Palsy

Watch and see what she has trouble with. Maybe she has a hard time cutting paper. You could hold the paper steady while she cuts it. Maybe she is always the last one in line. You could stay with her so that she doesn't feel all alone.

Did You Know?

▶ Every year, about 6,000 to 8,000 babies are born with cerebral palsy.

▶ People with mild CP can ride bikes, drive, climb mountains, and even go skiing.

▶ Special wheelchairs are built for playing basketball, tennis, and racing.

How to Learn More about Cerebral Palsy

At the Library: Nonfiction
Carter, Alden R., and Carol S. Carter (Illustrator).
Stretching Ourselves: Kids with Cerebral Palsy.
Morton Grove, Ill.: Albert Whitman & Company, 2000.

Nixon, Shelley.
From Where I Sit: Making My Way with Cerebral Palsy.
New York: Scholastic, 1999.

Pimm, Paul.
Living with Cerebral Palsy.
Austin, Tex.: Raintree/Steck-Vaughn, 1999.

At the Library: Fiction
Anderson, Mary Elizabeth, and Tom Dineen (Illustrator).
Taking Cerebral Palsy to School.
Valley Park, Mo.: JayJo Books, 2000.

Fassler, Joan, and Joe Lasker (Illustrator).
Howie Helps Himself.
Morton Grove, Ill.: Albert Whitman & Company, 1987.

Mikaelsen, Ben.
Petey.
New York: Hyperion Press, 1998.

On the Web
Visit our home page for lots of links about cerebral palsy:
http://www.childsworld.com/links.html

Note to Parents, Teachers, and Librarians: We routinely verify our Web links to make sure they're safe, active sites—so encourage your readers to check them out!

Through the Mail or by Phone

American Academy for Cerebral Palsy
and Developmental Medicine
6300 North River Road
Suite 727
Rosemont, IL 60018-4226
847/698-1635

Cerebral Palsy Information Central
c/o Anee Stanford
West Campus #104 ISU
Pocatello, ID 83209

Easter Seals
230 West Monroe Street
Suite 1800
Chicago, IL 60606
312/726-6200 or 800/221-6827
http://www.easter-seals.org

March of Dimes Birth Defects Foundation
1275 Mamaroneck Avenue
White Plains, NY 10605
888/663-4637
http://www.modimes.org

National Institutes of Health
Neurological Institute
P.O. Box 5801
Bethesda, MD 20824
800/352-9424
http://www.ninds.nih.gov

United Cerebral Palsy
1600 L Street, N.W.
Suite 700
Washington, DC 20036
202/776-0406 or 800/872-5827
http://www.ucp.org

Index

About the Author

Susan H. Gray has a bachelor's degree and a master's degree in zoology. She has taught college-level biology, anatomy, and physiology classes. In her 25 years as an author, she has written medical articles, science papers, and children's books. Gray especially enjoys writing on scientific topics for children, as it is a challenge to present complex material to young readers. In addition to her children's books, she writes grant proposals for several organizations. Gray lives with her husband, Michael, in Cabot, Arkansas. She enjoys playing the piano, traveling, and gardening.